Table of Contents

Introduction to Stable Coins 3
    What are Stable Coins? 5
    Why Stable? 6
    Roles of Stable Coins 7
    Storing Stable Coins 8
    GUSD (Gemini Dollar) 9
    USDC (USDCoin) 10
    TUSD (TrueUSD) 11
    PAX (Paxos Standard Token) 12
StableCoins in Other Countries 13
    Introduction to CryptoRuble (Russia) 13
    República Bolivariana de Venezuela:Petro 15
    Digital Token Stablecoin in Taiwan:TWDT 18
    Stellar Venture by IBM USD 24
    Simple Explanation of Dai Stablecoin Maker 29
    Payment Platform of Havven:Nomin USD (nUSD) 34
    Building Startups by Basecoin(Basis) 37
Conclusion 40

Book Description

This book emphasized greatly on the stable coins in the cryptocurrencies with learning their usage. The impact of each coin is special with helping to make the crypto world stronger than before. Not only US but there are other parts of the world which also use the stable coins in various forms. You will get to learn about various topics in this book mentioned below:

Introduction to Stable Coins

- GUSD
- PAX
- TUSD
- USDC

Stable Coins in Other Countries

- Introduction to CryptoRuble (Russia)
- República Bolivariana de Venezuela:Petro (COULD NOT FIND DATA FOR THIS)
- Digital Token Stablecoing in Taiwan:TWDT
- Stellar Venture by IBM USD
- Simple Explanation of Dai Stablecoin Maker
- Payment Platform of Havven:Nomin USD (nUSD)
- Building Startups by Basecoin(Basis)

Introduction to Stable Coins

The market of cryptocurrencies is expanding and being prominent significantly. It has acquired a mass market with attracting many people around the world. The appeal of cryptocurrencies through decentralization, low fees, no intermediaries and much more is impressive enough to compel anyone to join it. It becomes a major integration in the life of an ordinary man.

The ease of transferring the amount in the world of cryptocurrencies has become a piece of cake. Within seconds, you are able to do a transaction without knowing where it is going or to whom. The interaction with other is completely anonymous which makes it even more impressive for the people to interact through it. With the popularity of bitcoin, Ripple, Ethereum and other tokens, stable coin is one of the special cryptocurrency in the market.

When you talk about the institutions which are centralized, it becomes hard to transfer the money because of so many complications involved. The funds moving and the sending out the money which will take days to reach at the other end of the world. it can get quite disturbing for you to send money. Above that, you have to pay the fee for the wire transfer for the institutions which can be quite frustrating too.

You can lose a lot of money in sending out an amount across the border through the centralized institutions. Cryptocurrencies help you get rid of the obstacles which people face on daily basis.

You acquire the bitcoin at a time on a certain rate and the next time, you sell it to someone else instantly on another rate.

The speed of transactions is exceptional which is why dealing with numerous payments online can be easy for you through cryptocurrencies. The blockchain helps you to resolve any issues with receiving the payments. There will be less issues than before when you get used to of this system if you are an e-commerce business. You do not have to depend on the bank or worry about the spammers online as it is fully protected as well.

With the help of stable coins, every issue is going to be resolved. So let's get started with learning about stable coins not only within US territory but also at different parts of the world.

What are Stable Coins?

One of the popular cryptocurrencies are stable coins. They are the pegged total amount of all the other assets with the USD in most of the cases. Some of the popular ones are PAX, USDCoin, Gemini Dollar and TrueUSD. These are some of the ones which will be discussed in the following sections.

Why Stable?

Stable coins work as the bridge in the world of cryptocurrencies and the currencies fiat globally. The price volatility gets controlled through the centralized authorizes which are backing up the coins through USD or the cryptocurrencies. As an example, TrueUSD is one of the popular cryptocurrencies nowadays. Every token of TUSD has a backup with $1 as a proof which makes it published.

It is based on the ethereum blockchain and gets the protection legally through the third party audits and the holders of TUSD. However, if you talk about Paxos, it also works under the ethereum blockchain. It has the backdoor PAX authorities which makes the account freeze with allowing codebase.

Roles of Stable Coins

The problems initiating with price volatility and real world money made stable coins to take emerge. It solves out the problems within the markets related to pricing and the money which revolves in the real market. There are partnerships of stable coins with the companies to make sure that the costs remains same throughout in any case. There are no set limitations with crypto to USD for the redemption.

They are friendly for the customers so you do not have to worry about the rates associated with it. No one usually loses the funds due to changing of price however, the cross border payments will be convenient for them to manage with stable coins. The use of stable coins is usually to transfer the exchanges for bitcoin to USD.

Storing Stable Coins

Atomic wallet helps you in storing the stable coins without any hassle. You have to make use of the decentralized application which has multiple end support and the exchange which is built in the application. You can control the funds and no one else has the access to it.

GUSD (Gemini Dollar)

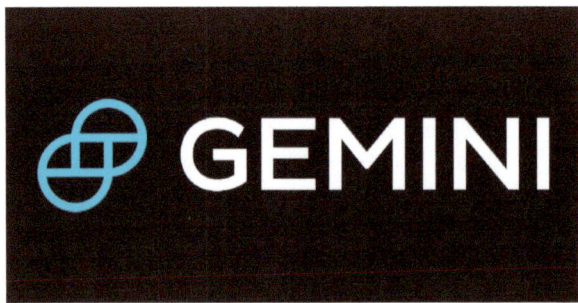

GUSD was established by the Gemini Trust Company which is based in New York. It is one of the first regulated stable coin which got approved in US and according to their regulations. It got built on the network of Ethereum with the 20 standard of 1 GUSD equals to $1. It is easy to manage and transfer GUSD through the platform of ethereum.

USDC (USDCoin)

The stable coin USDC is backed up by the US dollar. It got issued by the CENTRE by Circle. It is known to be the open source framework which offers solutions to the crypto market. The solutions are there to look into the operational and financial transparency which can sort out any problems in the cryptocurrencies. The regulation of framework are in the transmission laws operated with the banking partners and the established auditors. Any financial institution can join upon eligibility for the USDC. It is an open membership for the financial memberships if they are eligible for it.

TUSD (TrueUSD)

TrueUSD is the stable coin which is backed up by the ERC 20 standards and the USD. It gets exchanged through the multiple partners and have banking associations with the trusts. There are escrow payments involved through the legal identities which are collating with USD.

It holds a trust of the company with the account and the escrow payments. The smart contracts are there when it is about the clearance of the burns with the TrueUSD redeeming for the circulations of escrow accounts.

PAX (Paxos Standard Token)

Paxos trust company issued the PAX under the regulations of USA. It is under the particular services of finances in New York. It gets audited through the Withum which is an auditing firm and has the service monthly available. It gets redeemed through the US dollars one on on with the Paxos tokens available at the moment. There are audits which confirm the total USD and Paxos on monthly basis through these financial services.

StableCoins in Other Countries

Introduction to CryptoRuble (Russia)

Lately on the 7th of November, the State Duma Committee in Russia provided the details over the CryptoRuble. It was a long discussion under the cryptocurrency world and the government over these projects. The state backing along with stable coins has been equivalent through the fiat ruble within Russia. In the digital space, there are authorities which are backing up under the statements of contradictions. The ruble stable coins are not being stable at the end of the platform.

In the earlier times, Russia used to know cryptocurrencies as the bit ruble within their industry and later it became CryptoRuble for everyone to say it with the same name now.

The Story of Russian Cryptoruble Development

2015	Moscow-based WebMoney and Cyprus-headquartered Qiwi suggest to issue state-controlled digital currency to the Central Bank. The proposal is denied.
2016	Ministsry of Finance and Central Bank discuss a concept of national cryptocurrency
2017	Central Bank announces national cryptocurrency development. Vladimir Putin: "Cryptocurrencies cause serious risk and are used for crime". Unconfirmed reports on Vladimir Putin's strict order to develop "cryptoruble"
2018	The announcement of the Russian Association of Cryptocurrency and Blokchain (RACIB) launch scheduled for mid 2019. Vladimir Putin: "Russia cannot have its own cryptocurrency, as cryptocurrency "by definition" cannot be owned by a centralised state, since it "goes beyond borders". The announcement of the State Duma Committee on Financial Markets intention to launch state-backed cryptocurrency pegged to the Russian ruble

As viewed in the image the history of CrytoRuble is not so long ago. It was in 2015 when it started as the settlement payment system which was online. It had the headquarters in the Cyprus payment by Qiwi which later got approached through the CBR (Central Bank of Russia) issuing the currency control to the state or the country itself. The proposals were not accepted by the government initially as they were under the technical error and was considered illegal as well.

They were not known as the appropriate task for Russia to get started with nationally. It was considered as a disgrace to the currency of Russia to first emerge the CryptoRuble on the national basis. However, as the views changed later with the help of local officials, the concept modified for the government. There were minimization of anonymous transactions through the crypto world and the speed was tremendous to measure.

República Bolivariana de Venezuela:Petro

The currency of Petro introduced in February 2018 so you can imagine that it is not too long. It has not even been a year to this stable coin to be in the market. it is a part of crypto world under the government of Venezuela. The functions of the currency did not appear until the August of 2018. However, the country manages well between the minerals and the reserves of oil. There are currency issues which are accessible for the financing.

With the backup of the government, the financing options are there for the petro coins to have the value and gain control on it too. The president of Venezuela always wanted to have the backup with the reserves of oil. They wanted the sovereignty with the monetary issues and petro seems to be solving it out for them.

The new form of financing internationally helps their economy get better individually. Due to the economy of Venezuela, many other leaders doubted the fact that it will bring improvement in the system. They did not believe the concept of cryptocurrencies within the economy. However, the foreign debt of $140 billion compelled them to believe that it will make a difference.

There were 100 tokens introduced in the start of 2018 known as petro. These contain the value of $6 billion which acts as the best interest for the government and the economy overall.

The government helped in launching Petro in Venezuela in March with the tokens available instantly for the users. It had no audits independently which was initially stated in the white paper. The platform chosen for it was ethereum which is still the same till date.

Initially the platform was going to be NEM but they preferred to keep it simple and straightforward with Ethereum. The currencies manage to be under the schemes which are successful for the public and their tokens alongside. It helps them in launching the Petro sales which are up to 44 million worth the tokens.

Digital Token Stablecoin in Taiwan:TWDT

The Taiwan TWDT is based upon the technological corporation which is under the Green World Fintech industries. They announced their stable coins first time which is going to be named as the TWDT on the basis of ERC 20 standard tokens which will be operating on the ethereum network smoothly for the users.

The coin will have the peg in the Taiwanese Dollar for the system to keep some of the measurements. It needs to resist the fraud or any laundering in the money with the dollar conversion to the tokens as they should be patented. Along with that, the tokens will be online for the retails and the terminals to assist through the transactions.

Market for Stable Coins

The issues faced by the cryptocurrencies in the market have been the adoption for the people. they are not able to deal with the volatility of the prices in the market due to which stable coins have to jump in. they are making the payments and the transactions uncomfortable for the people to use on daily basis.

It leaves less room for the payment value along with falling next to the significant level. There are some of the solutions which can be there to fiat the cryptocurrencies through the general public involvement. It works as the conversions for some of the complications which are there for the support and the management.

However, with the commerce and the stable coins, they are able to win through trading and get gains over without having much cash on the pocket. The developments are there for the marketplaces to keep things under considerations with tokens and coins. Along with that, the benefit with minus and plus of the price will be there until the release.

The pegged coin is there to keep the cryptocurrencies under the markets. The platform of payment is backed up by the cryptocurrencies and that is the main aim of the Green World. it helps in sharing the market place with reaching up to 70 percent of the times throughout the country.

There are scams with the money laundering which will be minimized through the TWDT. The plan is to put the system patented through this stable coin so that no one is able to scam money. It also let the sales point to be under the terminals and specialized so that banks do not have to worry about it.

The verification of the customer is through their identifications cards and they are able to send the money through the trustable accounts. It is better to send the cash through transfer on the terminal point and keep it verified with the payment details. The processes are there with the effective system and laundering it up to the origin and the traceable points.

A foundation needs to be solid under the mining of this cryptocurrency in Taiwan. All the concerns with in the department have to be under the release before it is there to use by the people in the market. It helps sufficiently with knowing how there are comparisons within the market and what is the value of the public for these stable coins.

There are some of the measures which are adequate and need to be there with the system to keep it running smoothly and firmly. As there may be fluctuations in the price, there will be a time when the demand will increase as well.

It opens the doors for the dealers and the investors which makes the economy strong overall. There are many concerns which are revolving with the government yet to be addresses. The coins are there for the exchanges of the TD so the fears are legible for the people including the government.

Stellar Venture by IBM USD

The official network of Stellar is here after the effort of several years. It is backed by the anchor of USD which is issued by Stronghold. Recently there have been collaborations with IBM to check out the blockchain which is with USD stronghold. Among all the networks, it proves to be dynamic through the IBM blockchain how the platform is significantly available for Stellar.

Now with the help of US dollars, it is possible to bring on the assets which are holding back the network of Stellar for so long. The custodians of such as Prime Trust are there with the organizations known for the safer and efficient transactions globally which are faster as well.

The implications are strong and there are more people knowing about the community which are there on the blockchain. You have to know about all the information before investing in such stable coin.

The protocol of Stellar has been through multiple adoptions on the ethereum or bitcoin. There are many levels which had to be crossed in order to make accessible for the people widely. The network did not perform well as of playing a part just for itself for a while. With the exchanges of Coinbase, there was a chance that traders would invest in BTC or ETH.

The tradeoff did not go so well with the users because of the fees and the wait times which people had to go through. Anyone who has been planning to invest in Stellar had to be careful for the ETH and the BTC because they would have to convert it to the XLM versions.

The access for the wallets and the transitions was tradable with these ways throughout. For keeping the information to the next level, there has been the fiat and with the bank accounts, it felt easier to fill the gap between the currencies along the networks. The USD supported the idea for the Stellar and had to be an advantage for some of the networks which perform powerfully currently.

Stellar is known to be one of the best networks until now. It suits with the protocol of the people who are sitting across the border. They have to do transactions and there isn't any better way to do rather than the stellar stable coin.

You have to send the money to someone so why wait. There is no wait included with stellar as it is there for you to keep the time efficient. The XLM and people are there working as the traders for to take powerful advantage of Stellar. The table below shows the comparison which you can know through other networks. It helps you in analyzing why Stellar may be the choice for you among all the other networks.

PROTOCOL COMPARISON	Bitcoin	Ethereum	Stellar	Ripple
Average Transaction Confirmation Time	1 hour	15 minutes	3 to 5 seconds	3 to 5 seconds
Average Transaction Fees	$0.61 per transaction	$0.02 per transaction	$0.01 for 300,000 transactions	$0.01 for 3 transactions
Transactions Per Second	3 transactions per second	7 transactions per second	3000 transactions per second	3000 transactions per second
Consensus Mechanism	Proof of Work	Proof of Work	Stellar Consensus Protocol (SCP)	Ripple Consensus Algorithm
Validator Control	Decentralized	Decentralized	Decentralized	Centralized
Governance	Non-profit	Non-profit	Non-profit	For profit

Stronghold

Why USD?

Among all the other foreign exchanges USD is popular and known to have value around the world. Who does not like to have dollars in their accounts rather than their own currency? It has a value like no other currency in the world which is why people prefer to have it in their accounts instantly. Similarly, it is easier for the people to adopt the foreign currency when it is in the form of USD. They do not hesitate while doing the transactions as it can be keep the flow of speed smoothly and quick for the users.

Simple Explanation of Dai Stablecoin Maker

Dai is equal to $1 which is keeping Maker as the collateral system to work. It helps the price feed to manage by the MKR token and their holders are pretty satisfied with it. There are a lot of buyers which are working on the last resort to keep the MKR holders as the main buyers. The magic of blockchain is through the smart contracts which it has to offer for the users. However, settlement with the global system remains with knowing the safety needs and learning some of the final layers throughout.

With the stable coins, they are able to pull off the blockchain and its technology through realizing that there are some of the things which need to be decentralized. The leverage is there for keeping the performance up to the mark with having response time among the users.

The response of the management is through simplification which is in a fashion of writing things down not too complicated to understand. The parents work together it keeping things simple and without the technical understandings among the users. There are many details associated with it which are look upon despite any further understanding on it.

Product of Maker

The focus of Maker is to make the organization strong through Dai. Dai is the stable coin which is in the market recently and helps you in pricing of the transactions. It is basically a token which is used in the blockchain world to trade currency. It does not have volatility like other tokens like bitcoin or other coins. Dai assets are stable with keeping it relative to the market and under the US Dollars. With equally to one dollar, it sets up the consumer trade without any stable coin associated with it.

You are known to many other stable coins in the market which hold the bank accounts of US and are present on the blockchain platform. With keeping in mind, the tokens are there with backing up the cryptocurrency along with knowing some of the coins. There are bank accounts which should be under the accountants and keeping the holding systems for them. You have to keep the backups to make sure that the tokens are there with the insertions among the accounts.

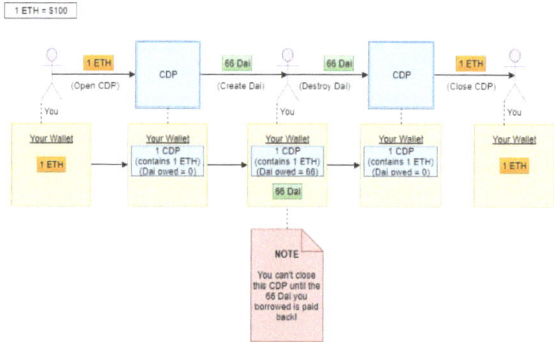

The tokens within the market have to be under the blockchain which is relying on the accounts. It is completely over the stable accounts which you have to keep systematic and trusted parties for it. The complete blockchain are there with keeping the mediators alongside. Many people think that they do not even need stable coins but that would be a wrong decision.

It will be viable that you gain access to the volatile blockchain which are under the nominations or the currency alongside. You have to keep the currency which is under the application and keeping the technology without having any promise or realization.

So to keep things short, it is better to allow the exchanges which are decentralized takeover the stable coins which people like to have it in daily lives. It makes the transactions convenient for the users with knowing that they do not have to wait any longer.

Payment Platform of Havven:Nomin USD (nUSD)

Havven Nomin USD is known to be a platform for the peer to interact with each other through the decentralized environment. It helps the users with the transactions and makes sure that they are able to do the transactions with the stability of price. They ecosystem stable coin Havven is known to be pleasant for some of the users online.

It helps in building up the mechanisms which are encouraging and help in collaborating with the systems. It facilitates the payments through tokens and keeps the stable connection within the accounts. There are transactions which are based on the fiat currencies alongside without any processing or the payments exchanging over blockchain.

How does it work?

It works on the ethereum blockchain which helps in keeping the backbone of the payment system. Basically it is a solution based stable coin which helps the economy and makes then produce the token system which is dual in its own nature. The system runs on the dual tokens to keep the collateral network and also goes through the payments in the convenient environment for the users.

With the help of token pay, there are transactions which are held with the value of Nomin only. The utilization of the decentralization is there with consistent value of resources. The rates are there for the cheaper side of the gateways which is why you have to keep the network smooth for it to be operational.

The token Nomin helps you in getting the medium to superior performance for the Havven stable currency. There are exchanges throughout the transactions which you have to go through which is why you have to keep the value in mind. However, in return, you will be able to find out about the main tasks which are there for you to keep in mind despite the normal nomination of the amounts.

If there is low demand, then it will be of the high value in the market. When the demand increases, there will be changes in the price as well. With the collateral image of Havven in the market, there are static changes which you may feel with the assets. New forms of the money and their representation may make you leave or eliminate some of the problems which you may be facing throughout the system. It will eliminate all the escrow payments which will be there to redeem later on.

Building Startups by Basecoin(Basis)

The logo of basis is loved by many people thinking that at least it's better looking. However, there are monetary policies associated with cryptocurrencies which you have to follow. The algorithms, simple games, bonds, violations and the volatility of the stakeholders which are a part of this stable coin.

Recently there was an announcement over the Basis known as base coin too which is around the funding of $133 million. There are many projects which are presently appearing but this will surely catch your eye if you are a part of blockchain. It helps in falling under the category of standards along with course central banks.

The expansion of the market is through the exchange rate system. It works fairly with the white paper along with wishing the team to have ecosystem on the stable side of the account. The potential look for it there for the investors and the users at both ends. It is better to keep the monetary policies with the currency over stable coin side.

With the prominent economy, it makes a difference when you are at the blockchain platform doing the transactions with people all around the world. The monetary policy of basis is known to be on the demands. The coins supply and its current usage of the plan keeps the currency stable for the basic shares.

It also holds the new supply with policy makers among the monetary terms. With keeping the system pumping for the exchange, there are demand increment with the additional sharing of the holders. There are receiving of the base coins within the market to keep it settled for the base coins.

However, when the system is about to fall off, the price decrease automatically with the expansion in demands. People think that it is about violating the policies but actually it is not. The money supply and demand is in the control of no one. You do not have the backup plan for it as the demand increases or decreases with time. There can be problems with the bonds knowing that it will never be enough for the holders to utilize it completely.

Conclusion

To keep the structure running on the blockchain, there has to be some of the new initiatives which keeps the users motivated. It helps them look into new insights so they can make use of it completely. The mode of transactions and dealing with the payments has been problematic for many countries including USA. Some of the major stable coins will help resolve the issues not only for US but other parts of the world as well.

They have the conversion rate accordingly with the US mergers which helps the accounts stay stable. As US currency is known worldwide and is known to be one of the valuable ones, it stands among all other currencies staying as the base for all.

Hopefully, this book helped you gain proper knowledge about the stable coins and how you can use them to make the blockchain platform more useful for yourself.